anything

D1062591

LAUGHING MATTERS

OUTDOOR JOKES

Compiled by Pam Rosenberg
Illustrated by Patrick Girouard

Special thanks to Donna Hynek and her second grade class of 2005–2006 for sharing their favorite jokes.

Published in the United States of America by The Child's World®
PO Box 326, Chanhassen, MN 55317-0326
800-599-READ
www.childsworld.com

Acknowledgments
  The Child's World®: Mary Berendes, Publishing Director

  Editorial Directions, Inc.: E. Russell Primm, Editorial Director and Line Editor; Katie Marsico, Managing Editor; Assistant Editor, Caroline Wood; Susan Ashley, Proofreader

  The Design Lab: Kathleen Petelinsek, Designer; Kari Tobin, Page Production

Library of Congress Cataloging-in-Publication Data
  Outdoor jokes / compiled by Pam Rosenberg;
  illustrated by Patrick Girouard.
      p. cm. — (Laughing matters)
   ISBN-13 978-1-59296-709-4
   ISBN-10 1-59296-709-4 (library bound : alk. paper)
   1. Animals—Juvenile humor. 2. Nature—Juvenile humor. I. Rosenberg, Pam.
  II. Girouard, Patrick. III. Title. IV. Series.
   PN6231.A5087 2007
   818'.60208—dc22   2006022655

OUTDOOR JOKES

Sherlock Holmes and Dr. Watson went on a camping trip. As they lay down for the night, Holmes said, "Watson, look up into the sky and tell me what you see." "I see millions and millions of stars." "And what does that tell you?" "It tells me that there are millions of galaxies and billions of planets," replied Watson. "What else does it tell you?" asked Holmes. "It tells me that God is great and that we are small and insignificant" said Watson. "Anything else?" asked Holmes. "Yes, it tells me that we will have a beautiful day tomorrow. What does it tell you?" Holmes replied, "It tells me that somebody stole our tent!"

CAMPING JOKES

One Sunday a camper went swimming in the river. When he wanted to come back on shore, he couldn't. Why not?

Because the banks are closed on Sunday!

What's green and short and goes camping?

A boy sprout.

How do hikers cross a patch of poison ivy?

They itch hike.

Counselor: Quinn, what are you going to do in the camp talent show?

Quinn: Imitations.

Counselor: Great, let me hear one.

Quinn: I love you—ouch! I love you—ouch!

Counselor: I give up. What are you imitating?

Quinn: Two porcupines kissing.

How do campers dress on cold mornings?
Quickly!

Why didn't the witch like to sleep in a tent?
Because it didn't have a broom closet.

Where do little dogs sleep when they go camping?
In pup tents.

How can you tell if there's an elephant in your sleeping bag?
By the smell of peanuts on his breath.

A camper fell out of a canoe in the middle of the lake. He didn't swim or sink. How could that be?
He floated.

Why did the boy put a frog in his sister's sleeping bag?
Because he couldn't find a snake.

5

Why did the camper put his tent on the stove?
He wanted a home on the range.

When does a camper go zzz—meow—zzz—meow?
When she's taking a catnap.

What do octopuses take on camping trips?
Tent-acles.

What happened when the silly camper bought a sleeping bag?
He spent three weeks trying to wake it up.

Can you start a campfire with one stick?
Yes, if it's a match!

How do you make a bedroll?
Push it down a hill.

What grows fast and goes camping?
A Boy Sprout.

When you are trying to tell stories around the campfire, why don't you want goats there?
Because they're always butting in.

A hiker went without sleep for seven days, but wasn't tired. What was his secret?
He slept at night.

What did the hiker say when she ran into a porcupine?
"Ouch!"

Camp Counselor: What are you taking home from camp—the train or the bus?
Camper: I don't think either one would fit through the door!

Two campers were playing checkers. They played five games and each won the same number of games. How is that possible?
They played against different people.

What happens when you hike across a stream and a river?
You get wet feet.

Linda: What would you get if you crossed a vampire and a camp counselor?
Russell: I don't know, but I wouldn't want to be in his cabin.

Caroline: Tommy's parents sent him to camp.
Katie: Did he need a vacation?
Caroline: No, they did.

What kind of camper do you get if you cross a porcupine and a young goat?
A stuck-up kid.

Camp Counselor: Andrew, get up! It's seven o'clock! The birds have been awake for hours.
Andrew: If I had to sleep on a tree branch, I'd get up early, too.

Josh: What do you get if you cross a gopher and a porcupine?
Megan: I have no idea.
Josh: A tunnel that leaks.

BUG JOKES

If ants are so busy, why do they always have time to show up at picnics?

What do you get if you cross a bee with a skunk? An animal that stinks and stings.

What did the bee say to the flower? Hello, Honey!

What's a mosquito's favorite sport? Skin diving.

What do you get if you cross an ant with a tick? All sorts of antics.

Where do bees go on vacation? Stingapore.

Two flies were in the camp kitchen.
Which one was the football player?
The one in the Sugar Bowl.

Why was the insect kicked out of the national park?
Because it was a litterbug.

ANIMAL JOKES

Have you ever hunted bear?
No, but I've been
shooting in my shorts.

What kind of bird
steals from banks?
A robin.

What is a duck's favorite TV show?
The feather forecast.

What animal uses a nutcracker?
A toothless squirrel.

Why do squirrels spend so much time in the trees?
To keep away from all the nuts on the ground.

What happens when ducks fly upside down?
They quack up.

What do you get when you try to cross a mouse with a skunk? Dirty looks from the mouse.

What do you call a very large moose? Enor-moose.

What's a frog's favorite flower? A croakus.

What happened when the owl lost his voice? He didn't give a hoot.

What's the best thing to do if you find a skunk in your sleeping bag? Sleep somewhere else!

What would you get if you crossed a rabbit and a frog? A bunny ribbit.

Ranger: How can you tell a boy moose from a girl moose?
Tenderfoot: By its moose-tache.

How do we know that owls are smarter than chickens? Have you ever heard of Kentucky Fried Owl?

Knock knock.
Who's there?
Owl.
Owl who?
Owl be seeing you.

Two hikers were sitting around a campfire when a huge grizzly bear came toward them.

"Keep calm," said the first hiker. "Remember what we read in that camping book. If you stay still and look the bear right in the eye, it won't attack you."

"I don't know about that," said the other camper. "You read the book and I read the book, but has the bear read the book?"

Girl Scout Leader: Why do bears live in caves?
Girl Scout: They can't afford apartments in the city.

Ranger: What would you do if a bear came after you while you were hiking though the woods?
Tenderfoot: I'd climb a tree.
Ranger: That's not smart; bears can climb trees.
Tenderfoot: Not this tree. It would be shaking too hard.

When should a mouse carry an umbrella?
When it's raining cats and dogs.

Knock knock.
Who's there?
Gopher.
Gopher who?
Gopher pizza, I'm hungry.

What do you get if you cross a parrot with a woodpecker?
A bird that talks in Morse code.

HUNTING JOKES

What fur do you get from a tiger?
As fur away as possible!

Tom: I'm going on safari to Africa.
Nate: Drop us a lion.

Nate: How's the safari going?
Tom: Safari so good.

What sort of music is played
in the jungle?
Snake, rattle, and roll.

FISHING JOKES

Teacher: Why did you go fishing instead of writing your book report?
Student: Book report? I thought you said "brook report"!

What did the football coach take with him on his fishing trip? His tackle.

Game Warden: Can't you read the sign? It says "No Fishing Allowed"!
Nicholas: Oh, it's okay. I'm fishing silently.

Game Warden: You fishing?
Patrick: Nope, just drowning worms.

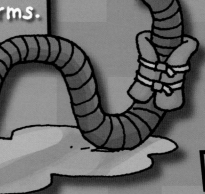

19

Pete had been fishing all day without any luck. On the way home he stopped at a fish market and said to the clerk, "Please stand there and throw me four of your biggest trout."

The clerk looked confused. "Throw them to you? Why?"

"I may be a poor fisherman, but I'm no liar," Pete replied. "I want to be able to tell my family I caught them myself!"

Game Warden: Don't you know you can't fish without a permit?
Anna: That's okay, mister. I'm doing fine with these worms.

Why couldn't Batman go fishing?
Because Robin ate all the worms.

Why did the silly football player bring a rod and reel to tryouts?
He heard the coach was looking for a tackle.

FOREST JOKES

What's the smartest tree in the forest? Albert Pinestein.

What home computers grow on trees? Apples.

Why did the tree pick up a book? To leaf through it.

What's brown and hairy and fights forest fires? A suntanned forest ranger who needs a shave.

What grows on trees and can lift very heavy weights? Hercu-leaves.

What's a tree's favorite drink? Root beer.

Why couldn't the tree answer the teacher's question? It was stumped.

OUTDOORSY TONGUE TWISTER

One worm wiggled while
Two tiny toads tasted tea while
Three thirsty turkeys thought while
Four frantic flamingoes flapped while
Five ferocious felines flashed their fangs while
Six slow sloths silently slept while
Seven stinky skunks started singing while
Eight elderly elks eloped while
Nine needlefish knitted napkins while
Ten tarantulas tapped tambourines.

23

About Patrick Girouard:

Patrick Girouard has been illustrating books for almost 15 years but still looks remarkably lifelike. He loves reading, movies, coffee, robots, a beautiful red-haired lady named Rita, and especially his sons, Marc and Max. Here's an interesting fact: A dog named Sam lives under his drawing board. You can visit him (Patrick, not Sam) at www.pgirouard.com.

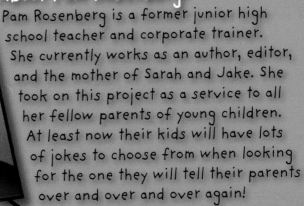

About Pam Rosenberg:

Pam Rosenberg is a former junior high school teacher and corporate trainer. She currently works as an author, editor, and the mother of Sarah and Jake. She took on this project as a service to all her fellow parents of young children. At least now their kids will have lots of jokes to choose from when looking for the one they will tell their parents over and over and over again!